The Supreme, Superb, Exalted and Delightful, One and Only Magic Building

THE SUPREME, SUPERB, EXALTED AND DELIGHTFUL, ONE AND ONLY MAGIC BUILDING

by William Kotzwinkle · Woodcuts by Joe Servello

Farrar, Straus and Giroux New York

Text copyright © 1973 by William Kotzwinkle • Woodcuts copyright © 1973 by Joe Servello • All rights reserved • ISBN 0-374-37303-5 • Library of Congress catalog card number: 72-96500 • Published simultaneously in Canada by Doubleday Canada Ltd., Toronto • Printed in the United States of America • Typography by Jane Byers Bierhorst • First edition, 1973

For Basho the poet and Hokusai the artist,
two old workers from long ago

A proclamation went out from the Emperor:

A MAGIC BUILDING IS TO BE CONSTRUCTED

Architects were thick as flies in the streets of the city, and they gathered in shops and on corners, waving their plans, shouting and arguing about who had the correct design for a Magic Building.

After seeing a thousand such designs, all of which failed to satisfy him, the Emperor came to a decision: "I am the only one fit to create a Magic Building."

Secluding himself in a lonely tower of his palace, the Emperor went to work, drawing and planning. Having seen so many schemes, he took the best features from each and incorporated them into one Supreme, Superb, Exalted, and Delightful Plan for the one and only Magic Building.

Stones and lumber were gathered. Only trees which had reached the age of one hundred years were suitable for use in the Magic Building—this was the Emperor's considered feeling—and there must be every type of stone and jewel included in its foundation.

The site for the foundation was a high plateau outside the Eastern Quarter of the Imperial City, and the ground was broken by the Emperor himself, with a gold pickax.

A hundred beasts of burden were brought to the site, along with a great force of workmen, one of whom was Old Ridgepole, the carpenter, who had brought himself out of retirement to appear at the great building site, carrying his battered old toolbox.

One by one, the craftsmen presented themselves to the Emperor for inspection. When Old Ridgepole stepped up to the royal table, the Emperor said, "Who is this decrepit old ruin?"

"Do not despise wood that is old," said Old Ridge-pole, "for it has weathered many a storm."

"Well," said the Emperor, "we might use you for sanding the Porch of the Seasons. I suppose you can't do much harm there."

The Porch of the Seasons was to have a green wall for Spring, a red one for Summer, gold for Fall, and white for Winter. Old Ridgepole went to work, with great patience, carefully sanding the lovely wood which had been brought from afar for the magnificent Porch.

Every day he rubbed, using all the different grades of his sandpaper, from rough to fine, back and forth, back and forth.

"Hey, old woodworm," shouted the Emperor, walking past Ridgepole's workbench, "you work too slowly!"

"Forgive me, Excellency," said Old Ridgepole, but he did not change his pace, for it was the speed at which he'd worked for many years, neither slow nor fast, but steady and sure. Every piece of wood he worked on became bright as a mirror, without bumps or holes, perfectly smooth all around.

"My wisdom has been proven," said the Emperor when the Porch of the Seasons was completed. "This surely is a most Magical Building. It shines in the sunlight like a jewel."

"Yes, Majesty," said the ministers of the court, "you are indeed a master builder." The court officials and the Emperor had a holiday on the wonderful glistening Porch, with music, food, and laughter.

The workmen spent the holiday in the huts which each of them had constructed near the site of the Magic Building. Among these crude dwellings, one in particular stood out.

Its rooftop curved gracefully upward at each corner like the wings of a bird. The walls were straight and finely joined, the door and windows beautifully shaped and sanded. This was the hut of Old Ridgepole, who spent the early morning hours constructing it and added little touches to it at the end of day, after his work on the Magic Building was through, for he did not want the hut to disgrace the site of such a marvelous structure as the Magic Building.

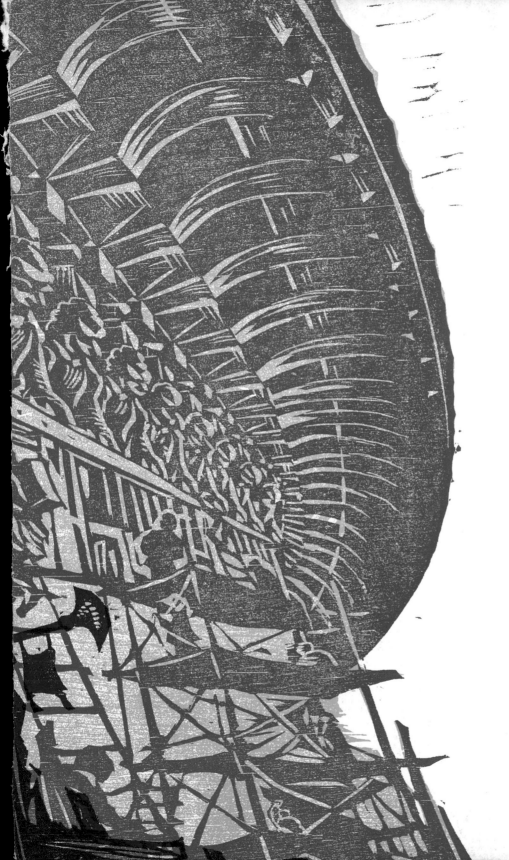

The second floor of the Magic Building was to be a great sacred dish, supported by twenty-four wooden dragons, representing the twenty-four hours of the day. The workmen lined up in front of the Emperor, awaiting their assignments.

"Well, old hammerhead," said the Emperor, "do you think you can sand the dragons without making too much of a mess?"

"The poor fool will try his best," said Old Ridgepole, and went to work with his various sandpapers, perfecting the rough countenance of the Hour Dragons.

The Emperor was delighted with the form of the bowl and the delicate finish of its shining dragons. "*This* is a Magic Building," he said to his ministers.

"Oh yes, Majesty," said the ministers, "even now the gods look down from their sky palaces with favor upon your Great Work."

"Hey there, old knothole," called the Emperor to the gray-bearded craftsman who was adding the last touches to the dragon eyes, "has there ever been such a magnificent palace as this?"

"No, Excellency," said Old Ridgepole, "never."

The highest floor was to show the twelve months of the year with twelve enormous wooden pillars made of giant trees from the highlands, each a thousand years old.

"I cannot trust such an old termite as you are with anything important," said the Emperor.

"Yes, Excellency," said Old Ridgepole.

"Well, make yourself useful at the sharpening stone," said the Emperor.

The forest was filled with the rasp of huge saw teeth as the lumbermen worked their way through the giant hardwoods. Smoothly did their blades go, and never bend, buckle, or stick, for Old Ridgepole knew how to make a saw sharp.

It took the time of twelve moons exactly to cut, haul, and fasten into place the twelve great pillars. By this omen the Emperor concluded that the work had progressed according to heavenly plan.

"Without doubt," he said to his ministers, "the gods look with favor upon my illustrious undertaking. Even with such nincompoops as this old doorstop"—he pointed to Old Ridgepole, who was mixing a pot of glue— "I have succeeded in raising a masterpiece."

That night, when the Magic Building was lit with many celebration lamps, thunder began to roll in the dark sky.

"The gods, Excellency," said the priests, "are themselves having a celebration in your honor."

The storm grew louder. Great winds blew. Like the voice of the dragon, the sky rumbled, and like a dragon's flaming tongue, great bolts of lightning lit up the night.

The Emperor sat on his new throne, and the floor beneath him trembled. He tried to drink a cup of rare wine, but the glass rattled so much the wine spilled down his royal chin. Those in the throne room looked around with nervous glances.

"There is nothing to fear," said the Emperor. "The gods are merely having a celebration in my honor."

The door of the throne room burst open with a cry of "Fire!" The room was rocked by a thunderclap of such intensity that the Emperor was tossed out of his throne. The ministers raced for the door.

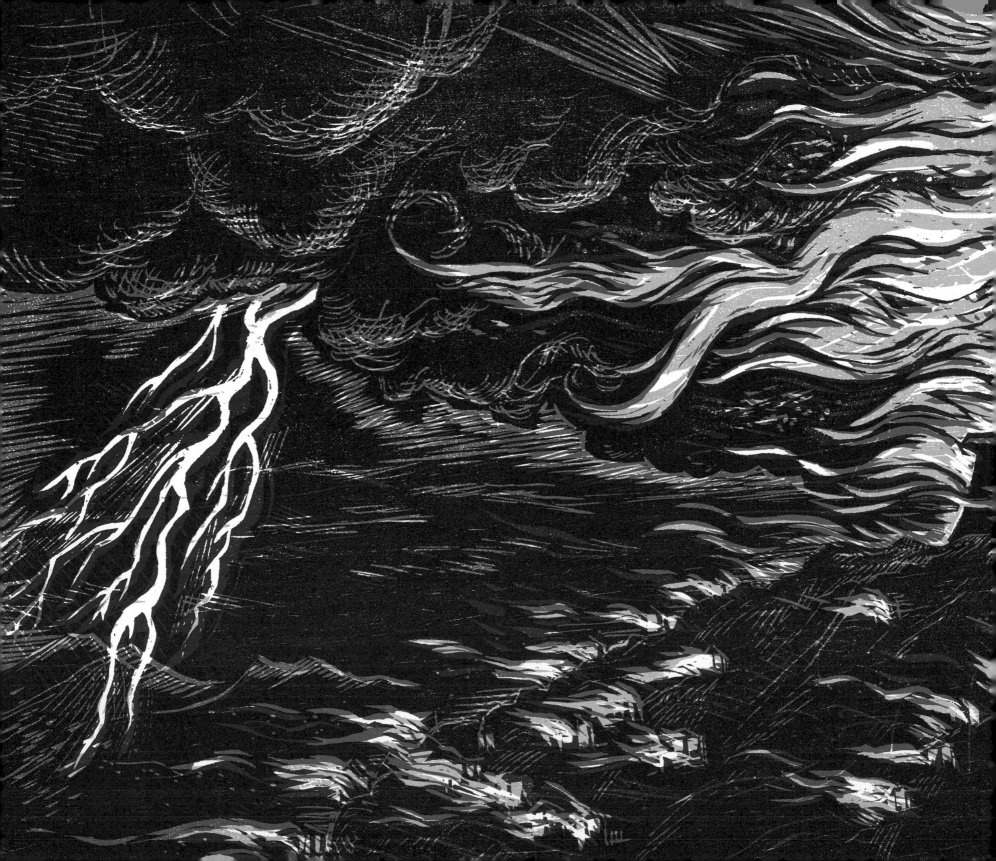

"Wait!" cried the Emperor, struggling to his feet. "This is my Magic Building!" He ran to the window. A bolt of lightning struck one of the enormous Pillars of the Moon, shattering it, as the other pillars groaned in anguish.

"Perhaps," thought the Emperor, "I had better get out of here." Down the jade staircase he ran, with flames licking at his gown, past the smoking Dragon Bowl of the Hours. Down he raced to the first floor, where the four faces of the year—Spring, Summer, Fall, and Winter—had become the flaming face of a witch.

Into the night he ran, and stood with his priests and ministers, workers and work animals, watching the Magic Building collapse and burn away.

Terrible winds drove the blaze beyond the Magic Building, into the workmen's huts, and those poor thatch-roof cottages burned like brief matches, one after another.

All day the sun shone brightly as the Emperor walked from floor to floor. Mysteriously flashing lights of many colors attended his movement through the Magic Building, and it was assumed these lights were the gods, in their celestial chariots, visiting and applauding the Emperor's achievement.

The workmen too were proud, though sad, for now that their work was done, they were not permitted to enter the Magic Building, as only those who were part of the Emperor's official court were fit to enter.

The Magic Building was finished. The Emperor stood at the portal, surrounded by priests and ministers, craftsmen and laborers, mules and horses. The sacred gongs were clanging and the Drums of Triumph rolled. "Now," said the Emperor, "I shall take the throne of Universal Monarch." Saying so, he stepped through clouds of incense, into the doorway.

Below, on every rooftop of the Imperial City, the inhabitants looked up in wonder at the Magic Building. No other country in the world had such a palace, leaping straight up to the gods.

When dawn came, the Magic Building was a smoking cinder. Beating the Drum of Sorrow, the people from the Imperial City came slowly up the mountainside and onto the plateau to view the ruin.

Untouched in the holocaust was the hut of Old Ridgepole. It stood in the debris, its roof still supported by the strong center ridgepole which the old carpenter had so carefully cut and put into place. As the sun rose upon it, it seemed to be glowing with a mysterious inner radiance, and all around it were seen flashing lights of red and blue, green and gold.

As the sun climbed above the mountain and shone down fully on the plateau, there fell a rain of dewdrops, sweet as the rarest fruit. These sparkling dewdrops covered the hut of Old Ridgepole, causing it to shine as if covered with diamonds.

The flashing lights gathered into a chain of lights, which now encircled the little hut, forming around it a glowing halo, like a rainbow of glorious colors. And the center of the rainbow, Old Ridgepole's hut, seemed to be made of gold.

The people let out a cry of wonder and delight, and called for the old carpenter to come out. The craftsmen gathered on all sides of the hut, saws and hammers in their hands, and clanked a curious music from their tools, until finally Old Ridgepole came forth.

The rainbow glistened behind him. In its lovely arc, the gods could be seen dancing and chanting, singing to Old Ridgepole.

He too seemed transformed. His gray beard was like silk, and his body was glowing with a mysterious inner light. He turned and addressed the rainbow, which became a bough of beautiful flowers, and perfume filled the air.

The priests came and bowed at the feet of the old carpenter, for they recognized that he was the Universal Monarch, and that the little hut he had built was the Supreme, Superb, Exalted and Delightful, One and Only Magic Building.

From his tiny palace of great purity, the thatch-roof hut of perfection, Old Ridgepole reigned, wise and learned.

The Emperor, whose three-hundred-foot-high building had so offended Heaven, put himself in the service of the old carpenter, who taught him through the years the proper, the perfect way to drive a nail.